CROSSING THE BORDER

COLLECTED POEMS

BY DANIEL A. OLIVAS

For Sue and Ben

Contents

Acknowledgments

I am not the first writer to consider poetry a form of storytelling. I draw upon many sources including my life (as in "Hot Tuesday on Rinaldi" and "Papa Wrote"), the lives of people I have had the honor of knowing ("Slip Dream" and "Why Did You Believe"), or news events ("Crossing the Border" and "Woman Gets Probation in Child Neglect Case"), to name a few obvious inspirations. Regardless of my poems' roots, I have many to thank for helping bring my first book of poetry to life:

Heartfelt thanks to Pact Press for understanding my poetic vision and accepting my manuscript as the press's debut title. May you sell many books!

Mil gracias to the wonderful writers Himilce Novas, Rigoberto González and Patty Seyburn who all offer kind words (blurbs!) in support of my book. Each of you has been an inspiration to me, and I deeply appreciate your selfless support of a fellow author.

I thank the editors of those lovely literary journals who bring poetry to readers and who first published many of the poems that make up this volume. Those journals are proudly acknowledged at the end of this book.

Over the years, I have become friends with so many writers, editors, educators, librarians, bookstore owners, and others who live in a world of the printed (and online) word. We are a community, and we are strong.

A special thanks to my parents, Miguel and Isabel Olivas, who made sure that their children had access to books. You instilled in me the joy of reading which is the first step to becoming a writer.

And, as always, I thank my wife, Sue Formaker, and our son, Benjamin Formaker-Olivas, who make my life joyous, meaningful, and delightfully crazy!

Crossing the Border

It's now a sport, great fun,
a diversion from your
work-a-day grind.

Hunt the mojados— "wetbacks" just
doesn't sound humane, now does it?
—as they run across the border from
Mexico to the great state of Texas.

Help the border patrol
(though they deny wanting help,
poor overworked bastards) by lining up
your pick-ups and jeeps (American-made,
of course) and shining your headlights bright and
revealing toward the scrub, toward
our neighbors to the south.

Share a nice little Jack Daniel's with
your buddy and keep a lookout for a
family or two, crouching, lurking,
hoping for a better life.

Cock your rifles, but never aim at 'em,
just blast a few warning shots
up into the star-filled,
moonlit night.

It's a beautiful evening,
redolent with desert life,

just waiting for them to
cross the border.

Papa's Car

Papa's car was battleship-sized—
a gray station wagon that creaked
and moaned with every turn.

Clear vinyl pulled tightly over the
seats revealing even more gray.
The rear seat faced backward
so that when I sat there, I could
see where I had been, but not
where I was going.

Papa's gray station wagon took
us places like Venice Beach, or
the dentist, or maybe a fiesta at
my school and or even to Abuelita's
house.

Sometimes we'd just drive, not
going anywhere in particular,
and I would fall asleep feeling
safe as Papa maneuvered our
ship through the vast ocean of
Los Angeles.

Las Dos Fridas

I would have been there
for you, when Diego was not.

But you were never alone,
you always had yourself.

The two Fridas, hand-in-hand,
waiting for no one yet hoping
for him.

But he is with a model,
a young, stupid, giggling thing.
That fat frog, forgetting his
true love to be in a puta's embrace.

I never would have forgotten you.

Never for a moment.

Es la verdad.

Letters to Norco

Dedicated to the incarcerated

My letters to Norco
kept you sane, you said.

Three years there for
selling meth. But I
wrote to you so you
wouldn't forget me.

And you wrote back.
Beautiful and sad letters.
Strong letters. But the
third one scared me
and then made me mad.
You told me that you
rented my letters
to your homies for a
quarter so they could
beat off to my sex-filled
longings where I told
you what my mouth could
do to your body and what
I wanted you to do to me.

But then I wasn't so mad.
And the thought of your
friends getting off from
my words made me smile.

12

So I made each new letter
even better, hotter than
the last. And when you
wrote back and told me
your homies loved my
words and that you could
charge thirty-five cents
now, I laughed at my
power.

And on your release day
as we stood in the August
heat outside the tall fence,
you held me and whispered
into my hair that we should
get married as soon as we
could and have lots of babies.
And you said my letters kept
you sane. And I said, me too,
mi amor. Me too.

St. Francis Dam, March 12, 1928

So, that cold night in March,
we stole a couple of horses from the ranch
where you worked, and started north.

It was the only way, you said,
to begin again, start fresh, commence
a life with possibilities.

And I agreed because I always did.
I always listened to my big brother.
I had no choice, did I?

After about an hour or two,
we heard something awful strange.
First, it started as a low rumble.

Couldn't figure out what it was.
Then it got louder and we felt it
in our chests like the rattle of influenza.

And we turned to look
out over the river,
in the direction of the St. Francis Dam.

We could see the outline of the
structure, designed and built by
the great William Mulholland.

L.A.'s chief water engineer back in '28, he

built that dam to hold two years' worth of water
in case an earthquake split the aqueduct.

We thought maybe it was an earthquake.
But what we saw made us stop
breathing.

The dam shifted and broke apart, crumbling.
The noise of the water—two years' worth, mind you—
shook our bodies and the horses' bodies, too.

Then we saw it: a wall of water,
ten stories high going into the valley
and rushing toward us.

I yelled, "¡Chingao! Let's get out of here!"
You just stared at the water, and you
froze, keeping your horse as still as you could.

I saw that you were thinking
about Juanita and your eight children
who slept in the shadow of the coming water.

I yelled again and you finally heard me
and we made those horses run
faster than they ever had before.

We rode until morning.

About five hundred people died that night
though more perished because many

15

migrant farm workers weren't accounted for.

We learned later that the water washed
away whole towns: Castaic and Piru,
anything near the river.

Sirens and phone calls alerted people
to try to outrun the water. Some made it.
Many did not.

Three hours after the dam broke, Santa Paula,
over forty miles away, lost three hundred homes
though most folks had already abandoned them.

And Saugus got hit so bad.
Totally destroyed.
Sad stories, too.

Like those forty-two children
Who'd been attending the Saugus Elementary School
were washed away, just like that.

The names of everyone who died,
or at least everyone who could be identified,
were listed in the California papers.

So, I tried to hide the *Los Angeles Times*, but
you found it and scanned the column with the headline:
PARTIAL LIST OF PERSONS DEAD.

I watched your dark eyes,

darting back and forth,
a frantic pace, searching for the names.

And I knew that you would find
halfway down the first column:
MRS. J. CARRILLO AND EIGHT CHILDREN.

Your knees buckled,
and I caught you.
I held you.

You wanted a new life.
So, we stole a couple of horses that
cold night in March.

I had no choice, mi hermano.
You always led.
And I always followed.

King

He tells me that the thrill is gone.
It's gone for good, he growls.

He should know because
he *is* the King.
My man B.B.

Even though my own marriage
is just fine,
thank you very much,
he makes me remember
a time long ago
when I was still single and hopping
from one woman to another
like a bee in a garden.

When the thrill slipped away,
silently, without a sound,
I would shake my head and
remember B.B.'s words.

The thrill is gone.

But you push on because there's
always another thrill out
there in the cool Los Angeles night.

And if you're lucky with the stars
glittering for you and only you, the thrill

will stay and you will sleep the sleep
of tired children.

The King knows this.

And in his noblesse oblige,
he tells us, in his way, that this is life.

Tezcatlipoca's Glory

I made a fool out of you
Back in the bright days
Of the Aztecs and Toltecs.
I made a fool out of you,
And it was easy.

I was a simple god,
Not as wonderful as you,
The great Quetzalcoatl.
¡Ay Dios mío!
You, the sun god, were the greatest!

Long after the Spaniards
Evicted us and brought the Christian
Deities, you were remembered!

Even D. H. Lawrence named
A novel after you: *The Plumed Serpent.*
Because that is your form,
A horrendous snake
With a head framed in magnificent feathers.

Yet who am I, simple Tezcatlipoca,
As compared to you?
The god of the air!
The pinche goddamned air!
What kind of god is that?

But it was I who shamed you

So that you fled Tenochtitlán,
Our homeland,
In humiliation.

I know you remember the night
I disguised myself
As a great hairy spider and
Offered you your very first taste of pulque
Which (as I'm sure you now know)
Is worse than tequila
Because it sneaks up on your brain
Without warning.

¡Ay! You got muy borracho!
And you loved that warm feeling
That ran down your throat and into your stomach
And your groin grew hot, too!

What did the great sun god do?
In a drunken heat,
You had your way
With your sister, Quetzalpetlatl!

I watched from behind a cactus
As you ripped her clothes, and you
Moaned an ugly moan, and your sister
Screamed and I laughed!

And in shame, you left your home
And wandered,
Leaving it all to me!

My brilliant plan,
So simple but so effective.
Why you would trust a great
Hairy spider is beyond me.
Perhaps your hubris lulled you
Into a sad belief that no creature
Would dare cause harm to Quetzalcoatl!

I made a fool out of you
Back in the bright days
Of the Aztecs and Toltecs.
I made a fool out of you,
And it was easy.

The House

Rosana bore Raúl six children in eight years.
The house creaked under the rambunctious
boys and girls,
three of each.

Rosana
died
with
the
last
child,
Isabel.

Isabel grew to be a sullen young woman
with deep eyes and hair the color of sorrow.

Raúl loved her
but knew that
she blamed herself for
Rosana's death.

One night,
at the age of fifteen,
Isabel packed a little bag,
kissed her sleeping father,
and left forever.

When Raúl
woke,

he knew in
his heart that
he was
alone.

And the house creaked as he wept into his hands.

Western Wallflower

Our little taste of the wild
atop the cement and
asphalt north of Ventura Boulevard,
in the summer heat of the
San Fernando Valley.

An inflorescence of orange-yellow,
each a lancet basal,
stems slender and arcing,
carpeting the vacant lot near
the sweaty hum of Valencio's Car Wash.

A breeze enhances their splendor,
incoming tide of old ivory hats
and long, cheerful, verdant legs.

Mustard is beautiful and native but,
when the eye approaches, street
loud and busy, you will see that it is
nothing more than a weed.

Papa, look at the beautiful flowers!

Yes, mijo, the flowers are gorgeous,
aren't they?

Can we pick some?

No, no. I smile, thinking the word *weed*.
No, no. Let them stay in nature.
They're happy there.

Pico Boulevard, October 1972

On Pico Boulevard it is hot, too hot, and smoggy
for October as bodies, large and small, stream out
of St. Thomas the Apostle Church.

"¡Ay Dios mío! That priest, that priest!" says Mrs.
Fonseca. "He cannot speak Spanish worth a damn!
When are we going to get a Mexicano to say mass?"

The stray, yellow dog barks near the votive candles
looking for attention and the children laugh as
they run to the empty lot three blocks down and
two over. "Shit, Alfredo! Stay away from me, you
pendejo! I'm gonna kick yo' ass, you pinche pendejo!"
Alfredo throws a stone anyway and laughs hard.

"Adriana, I understand your pain! My first grandbaby
came before the wedding, too! But it will be fine."

The siren shrieks as the gleaming red fire engine
streaks down the bustling street toward black smoke.

"Come on, Mirabel. I love you, es la verdad! You can't
question that. But I've waited long enough, haven't I?"

The siren is far off now, at its destination, firemen
helping the helpless, another tragedy confronted.

"Fifteen thousand dollars! Can you believe it!
in one fucking year! Selling this shit will keep

me in dinero better than any pinche college
degree. Hear me, Simón? Better than any pinche
Harvard. What? Shit, man. Don't give me that!
I've got it wired, man. Wired. Hear me? Wired!"

Hurt feet, too much perfume, rattling noise: honks,
laughter, coughing, cussing, cooing, church bells.

"Mi amor, what do you mean? You have my heart,
you know that! My heart! Believe me. I am not
lying to you. You are a wonderful husband, mi amor,
the best, es la verdad. I love you, mi amor. I do."

On Pico Boulevard it is hot, too hot, and smoggy
for October as bodies, large and small, stream out
of St. Thomas the Apostle Church.

A Good Job

"Come, D—,
get in.
It's just for
a few hours.
Six, max.
I promise."

D— looks
at his mother's
face.

"Here?" he
whispers.

His mother's
eyes dart about.
"Take this bag of
Doritos and two
7-Ups. Just a few
hours, D—. Okay?
Mama's gotta'
work."

"Okay," he says.
The boy climbs
into the trunk
of the old, white
Camry.

"Just for a few
hours, baby."
D— nods and
clutches the
bag of chips.

She closes the
trunk slowly
and pushes hard
until it clicks.

"Mama loves you,"
she says as she
walks down the
street to the glass
and steel building
on the corner.
"Mama loves her
big boy."

Green Soldier

The green soldier
could not stand.

Imperfectly molded, a thin,
sneaky wisp of plastic sprung
from his base so that he teetered
and tottered and fell if I tried to play
with him.

With a bit of a whine
if truth be told, I asked Mama to
fix him because he was my favorite,
better than all the other green
soldiers in my shoe box.

She put down the *Los Angeles Times*
and whisked my soldier off to the
bathroom.

Mijo, stay here, she
said. I'll be right back.

A moment later, I heard a
scream and my four-year-old
heart leapt.

Papa ran, frantic and confused,
from the bedroom to Mama.
The razor blade, her tool to fix

my soldier, had slipped and
sliced, deep and red, into her
thumb.

But my soldier could
now stand, proud and tall, and
I played with him as my sister
watched over me while Papa drove
Mama to the emergency room.

And my sister shook her head
as my green soldier
entered into a great,
heroic battle on the
turquoise, vinyl couch.

Lindy

We were drinking to that Lindbergh fellow
who landed in Paris two days before,
all the farm workers and ranchers stuffed
in that hot bar called THE TIN ROOF.

Dust and sweat and Prohibition booze
choked the air that stood as still
as a dead calf except for the swirling smoke.

So proud, so proud,
even though we wondered
how life in California
would be different.

But all of us Mexicans,
and the Chinese, too,
toasted him.

We lifted our glasses and cheered *Lindy!*

The papers said his mother was so proud
she couldn't find words to express her joy.

And President Coolidge declared
that he crowned the record of
American aviation.

They escorted Lindy,
like a handsome prince,

to the embassy after landing
and fighting the churning crowds.

Pats on the back, crying babies,
swooning women, and cameras, too—
Over here, over here!
One for the papers back home!

But Lindy's skin
was rank and sticky
from the flight.

So, the grinning American Ambassador's son
took the bone-weary aviator to a room at the embassy
where a beautiful, scorching bath waited.

Before dipping into the tub,
as steam filled the room,
Lindy gently drank some port
chased with a frothy glass of milk.

Papers said he relaxed for a real long time
(soaking and melting in sublime triumph)
before he got out,

combed his wild hair,

   slid on a pair of silk, flowered pajamas,

      draped his shoulders with a silk bathrobe,

         and tipped his toes with Moroccan leather slippers.

And he gave a few
charming interviews,
teeth shining white,
relaxing fresh and
clean, swathed in luxury.

I will never forget the night
we drank to Lindy, a hero,
who flew a plane while
we worked the fields
during a hot May, 1927.

Lindy! we cheered.
Lindy!

¡Los mejores son los que
se van primero!

Gato

My abuelita calls
Susie, my Siamese cat,
a "gato" which is just
another sneaky word for
"cat." Because gatos
and cats are sneaky,
don't you know?

I learned a long time ago
that cats are sneaky
with their love. Susie
could take me or leave
me depending on her
needs.

When she drowses
on the warm television,
eyes shut tight,
chocolate-dipped toes,
nose, ears, and tail twitching
in a dream of chasing pigeons,
I don't exist, and I
better not bother her or
else she'll growl like a dog.

But when Susie is hungry
or bored or wants
to be scratched, she
shows her love like

no one else could,
purring as she rubs
her furry sides so hard
against my legs that
I lose my balance.

My love is not sneaky.
But if it were, it'd be
sneaky like Susie's
love. Because even
sneaky love is still
love.

Barrow's Goldeneye

inlets and harbors
are your homes

with succulent shellfish
as your salty feast

sometimes you whistle
the wind playing games

with your wings so you
are called whistling ducks

by some who know
who you really are

your head sheens green
in the morning light

male and female
bear different marks

a shoulder bar here
a white crescent there

narrow white collars
bright golden eyes

little differences
little matter because

you are the same
you and your mate

as you slice through
cold waters side by

side as the yellow
sun warms your backs

The Brown Bomber

In Memory of Ernest Alderete, Sr.

Pop's chestnut skin glistened, tight and strong as he dove into Venice Beach's foamy waves and then shot up like a mortar and yelled, "I'm the Brown Bomber!" This was his favorite beach line.

So, for years, whenever I heard the Brown Bomber mentioned, I figured everyone just knew Pop. I mean, he was brown and he fought in Korea as a Marine. He eventually admitted that other men were also known as "Brown Bomber" (like the great Joe Louis), but there was another one who still lived in Monterey Park not too far from us.

The Brown Bomber: A war hero, my Pop said, who couldn't wait for his amphibious vehicle to reach the cold, dark Normandy shore. The way Pop told it, the Brown Bomber liberated dozens of death camps almost single-handedly.

But the Brown Bomber's second life, after the war, made my eyes widen and my teeth click with excitement. The Brown Bomber helped make a movie! And not just any movie. He's the one who, through celluloid trickery, made the swarming black ants in *Them!* look huge—bigger than a house—so they could eat everything from El Paso to L.A.

But the Brown Bomber died at the dawn of the new millennium. Killed not by a bullet or giant ant, but by the ordinary course of time at a commendable, wintry age. His daughters sprinkled his ashes along Yosemite's dusty hiking trails, which he helped build under the New Deal.

So, I guess Pop could borrow that moniker now. It's free to use. I'm sure the real Brown Bomber wouldn't care. Not really. Not anymore.

Hot Tuesday on Rinaldi

A poem concerning the shooting at the
North Valley Jewish Community Center

We stood on Rinaldi,
a hot Tuesday,
not knowing if you were
dead or
injured or
just scared.

A parent's ugliest nightmare
coming to us from the
radio while
we worked in our offices.

A shooting at the summer camp—
semi-automatic rifle,
over seventy rounds spent,
a white male dressed in
Army fatigues,
wanting to kill Jews.

Black asphalt where
SUVs and Hondas and Mercedes
usually rumbled
now cordoned off by yellow tape
while helicopters filled the summer sky
like locusts.

Rinaldi was a street
that was now ours
to roam
and wonder
and cry.

Three and a half hours,
we did not know,
and the perspiration dripped from
our faces and the
other parents
cried and yelled and whispered
while the police and
firefighters and
news people
outnumbered us three to one
in a circus of nausea,
TV cameras, and
disbelief.

We were finally
reunited, and your
Mama broke down
in shakes and quakes of tears
and your Grammy could not speak
and I could not feel.

You are a Jew.
You are Chicano.
You are our son.
And you are alive.

But much of your innocence
died that
hot Tuesday
on Rinaldi.

Outside the Box

Your words slide through the air,
and then hover before me, familiar but
strange, a different tongue,
an unlocked cipher.

My kid sister (if she were here, listening)
would laugh and say that I lack the facility
to wrap my mind around what you're saying
because, she would add, men can't think
outside the box.

I would look into my sister's
chocolate brown eyes
(God, she looks like Mom!)
and say, how do you know?
And she would point her thin finger at me,
an inch from my nose, and say,
don't go there.

Maybe a woman can understand a woman
when a woman is ending things with a man.
Perhaps this is an eternal truth.
Maybe men are out-of-the-loop
(as sis would say), hopelessly clueless.

And I admit that your reasons for leaving me
simply roll, clatter, and bounce around
my head like a cracked cat's eye in an
empty cookie tin, the kind with the

Christmas scene (sleigh, galloping horses,
snow, a Dickens' family of four)
embossed on its lid,
and on its sides, too.

Maybe, after some separation,
we can try again, you say,
hand on my shoulder like a football coach
gently cutting a hopeless but
good kid from the team.

No, I say, no.
I pull away,
your hand drops,
a dead weight.

You search my eyes,
and you see I finally understand
the truth beneath your words.

No, I say again.
Been there, done that,
as my sister would say.

Sad Gray House

Our sad gray house creaks and moans in the hot Los Angeles sun like a tired elephant waiting to die. I've made a nice brown puddle with a trickle from our leaky hose and Mama shares chisme with Rolando's mom across our chain link fence.

As I plunge my battered G.I. Joe into the homemade swamp, I hear Mama's tongue cluck, sharp and angry, while she hears how our chubby and happy priest has been sent away because he got caught with some pictures of a couple of altar boys.

I don't know what the big deal is. It's nice to have pictures of your friends. And that priest has so many friends. Friends like Claudio and Enrique from school. And me, too.

But he's gone now, some place far away like Orange County, and Mama just shakes her head the more she hears while bubbles rise up from my drowning soldier.

West Coast Jazz Marriage

A poem built upon 13 jazz titles by west coast artists

Yes, it is true:
I am way out west,
Though I admit that
You'd be so nice to come home to.

So,
My funny valentine,
I'll catch the sun
Because
You make me feel so young,

And because
It's a walkin' thing,

And because I
Look for the silver lining
On green dolphin street,

And because
All the things you are
I want,

You will see me soon,
Wearing my powder-blue tux,
Holding a little, gold ring,
Ready to tie that ding-a-ling knot.

So,
Cast your fate to the wind
And get into
A light groove.

But before I go,
I need one more drink,
One for my baby
(and one more for the road).

Do not worry, my love.
I can hold my liquor
And just to make certain,
I'll ask Joe to
Get me to the church on time.

Thanks to: Dave Brubeck, Art Pepper, Hampton Hawes, Chet Baker, Gerry Mulligan, Benny Carter, Barney Kessel, Ray Brown, Shelly Manne, Vince Guaraldi, Sonny Rollins, Cal Tjader, Sonny Criss and the Gerald Wiggins Trio.

Why Did You Believe?

Why did you believe
that he could be what
I am to you?

Slouching, laughing
too hard, teeth too white,
not really understanding
what you say.

A jerk of the head,
he sees another
curved lip,
another
rounded hip.

Vacant eyes pass you,
lost in other thoughts,
but you don't care
because he's what
looks right to other eyes,
eyes of your friends,
parents, strangers.

But it will end,
you know that's true
(deceive yourself if you must,
but for a moment),
it will end.

It will end.

Then will you believe the truth?

Writer

Writer? she asks. Do you write?
I blush and pull my thumb-worn

copy of *Poets & Writers* off the
counter, away from the cash

register, and push the video to
her. Well, kind of, I stammer.

I guess you can say that I do.
She smiles, takes the video and

scans it with her Star Wars laser,
across the bar code. Cool movie,

she says, forgetting her last query,
the one that startled me, made me

think about what I do late at night
after a long day drafting briefs or

making court appearances or
consulting with clients about

potential liability, chains of title,
inverse condemnation, environmental

reports, and the like. Yes, I do write
late at night when the day's ambitions

bounce and swirl in my head, I
should have said without hesitation.

Yes, I write. I'm a writer and I'm
glad you wondered, glad you asked.

¡Xicano!

It began as a cruel
Jibe (so the etymologists say)
Because the descendants
Of the great, fallen
Moctezuma could not
Purge their mouths of
The indigenous sounds of
Nahuatl, their mother tongue.

They worked the fields,
Almost slaves, but not
Quite, and called themselves
"Mesheecanos"—and the
bosses laughed.

Can't say Mexicanos?
Your tongues can't wrap
Around that, eh? Well,
Can you pronounce Chicanos?
Ah! So you can! That's
What you are!

Yes, that's what we are.
And guess what? We
Embrace it. And we can
Even dress it up further
By spelling it with an X
To bring us closer to
Those who came

Before us.

¡Xicano!

How does that sound to
Your ear? Does it hurt?
Does it make you shiver?
It does? So, sorry!
We don't mean to offend.
Please accept our apologies.
Have a nice day.

Slip Dream

When she said the words,
that odd phrase, one that
I'd never before heard,
I stopped talking, smiled,
repeated her words:

Slip dream.

The sun shone through,
hard and bright, bathing
the soft/safe earth tones
of her office, another
scorcher beginning outside,
a hot summer, one for the
record books.

What a fine term: slip dream.

She had told me to experiment,
try not to drink for a month,
see how I felt.

That's after going through the
family history: drunks going
every which way on the tree:
backward,
sideways,
forward, perhaps.

Runs in families, she said.
And you have it in spades.
But you're not like the
falling down alcoholics:
just one drink gets you
loose, thinking destructive thoughts,
not safe things to have in one's
head (I won't bore you with the
specifics: you've got your own
demons, right?).

So, take a month
vacation from the drink,
she softly suggested
with a smile.

Not a big deal, I thought.
I only have that one little
drink (maybe two) at night,
watching the news.
So what's the big deal.

But it felt odd
not having that drink.

And on the third night of
denying myself of that little treat,
I had the dream:

There I was, getting ready for work,
necktie neatly in place,

shirt crisp and immaculate
fresh from the cleaners,
and I grab a cold bottle of beer,
twist the top open with a hiss,
and take a big, wonderful swallow!
No, not something I normally would do.
I don't drink in the morning, ever.
So, in my dream, I feel stupid, like
a fool, and I pour the beer, amber
and beautiful, down the drain.

Ah! she said, even
before I could finish:

A slip dream.

She smiled a broad smile.
She had studied this long ago
in grad school, before getting
her license.
Classic, she said.
Pure textbook.
Excellent!

And I smiled.
What a perfect phrase.
Poetic, in its own way.

Yes, that's what I had the other night.
A slip dream.

Will I have it again tonight?
Will it become my little
secret as my wife sleeps
soundly by my side?
My small piece of fear,
guilt, all to myself?

What They Do

They come and go like
selfish, haughty felines,
mewing softly, speaking
their own special language,
waiting for someone to
translate, waiting for that
special phrase that says it
all, in a perfect capsule,
one that you can swallow,
easily, without hesitation.

Georgina S. Francisco is
a Friend of Mine

Georgina S. Francisco is a friend of mine,
and she is very particular about
two things: cheese and Margaritas.

"Cheese," she purrs, "must be strong,
sharp and sweet, like dulce."

She leans into me for emphasis.
"¿No?" she says through a red
O of a mouth.

"And there is only one way," she whispers,
"to make a Margarita."

I wave her off, my eyes bulging with
excitement, and tell her about my
latest Google search where I unearthed
the most remarkable Margarita recipe that
includes a bottle of beer.

Georgina's eyes narrow into mere slits,
and she spits out a disgusted, "Feh!"

Before I can say more, she stands and
looks down at me with disdain.

"There's only one way to make a Margarita,"
she sneers. "And it does *not* include beer."

Georgina turns on her heel leaving me
desolate with nothing more than her
perfume's scent and her rebuke's sting.

Georgina S. Francisco is a friend of mine,
and she is very particular about
two things: cheese and Margaritas.

Sisyphus Explains

They laugh
or cry
at my "plight"
that I need not
describe.

But, in truth,
this is great pleasure
for me, nothing less.

I am known for
my grand cunning,
great hubris, and
ferocious thirst
for power.

But this hill,
this stone,
this eternal
toil are all part
of my plan.

Tartarus is hilly
and charming, far
from my petty
concerns in Corinth.
So I am free to ponder
life's great mysteries
as I repeat my simple

and predictable
employment.

Do not cry for me,
Glaucus, Ornytion,
Thersander and Almus.
Treat each other well,
my sons, and
know that I am
at peace,
that I am well.

Wonder Bread

As my red wagon
shook and rattled
over the broken,
hot sidewalk, the
empty bottles bounced
and clinked and sang.

7-Up, Dr. Pepper,
Pepsi-Cola, and Tab.

A&W Root Beer,
Mr. Pibb, Fanta,
and Mama's
favorite: Fresca.

Three blocks to
Joe's Liquor where
Sam (I never met
Joe) would smile,
gold-capped teeth
glistening, a mouth
worth so much more
than my empties.

But the nickels he
counted out carefully
guaranteed that I
could walk to the
front aisle and grab

a pillow-soft loaf of
Wonder Bread.

This great transaction
(or ritual, if you will),
promised to end in
bologna sandwiches
for lunch under our
avocado tree this
perfect summer day.

Woman Gets Probation
in Child Neglect Case

They found you,
alive, yes, but
nude, caked with
dried ketchup
and jelly, lying
in a baby's tub
watching TV.

What did your
two-year-old
mind think as
you wandered
the house alone
for almost three
weeks? As you
peed on the floor,
scavenged for
food, drank water
from the toilet,
did you know that
your mother was
in jail, that she
didn't want to tell
the judge that she
had a daughter
who would need
care while she
served her time?

Did your mind
wander from
Sesame Street
to the dark
stillness of the
night to the
thirst you needed
to quench?

Will you remember
this time alone or
will your life be
filled with other
memories?

Your mother is
home now,
receiving only
probation instead
of the maximum
ten years. Your
mother is home
now, to fill
your life with
new memories.

Will I read about
you again as I
drink my morning
coffee? Will your
mother make

another headline
as my son sits
across from me
enjoying his
Pop-Tarts and
laughing at the
funnies? Will
I have to explain
again to him
why my eyes
have filled with
tears?

Papa Wrote

The crowd at Tía Chucha's
was sparse but smiling,
encouraging, waiting for
me to read a story or two.

I asked them to wait a few
minutes longer because my
father was late, and he had
promised to attend. And so
we waited in awkward
silence, the espresso machine's
hissing offering the lone
commentary.

And we waited,
and waited.

So we had to start. I opened
my book and read slowly,
assuredly, my words filling
these strangers' minds.

Halfway through, the front
door creaked open and my
Papa nodded, found a chair
in back. I smiled and everyone
knew who this man was.

I finished the story,

a gentle clapping
the final punctuation.
Time for Q&A I said.
A young man raised
his hand, asked a kind
question, a softball,
easy to answer.

My father then stood,
hands behind his back,
as I noted to the audience
that this is the man I had
been waiting for.

And Papa said:
"I used to write, too."

The audience nodded,
smiled, not knowing
where this was going.
Beads of perspiration
covered my upper lip,
my face frozen with
uncertainty.

"But it was trite,"
he continued.
"Nothing important."
He waved his hand,
palm out, as if to
wipe away the past,

to make certain we
understood.

Papa paused, cleared
his throat. "Nothing
like what you write."

"I wish I could read
your stories," I said.

Softly, he answered:
"I burned them all."
He smiled, without
sadness, and sat.

My Papa wrote, once,
long ago. He wrote
stories. Stories I will
never read. Stories I
will never know.

Hidden in Abuelita's Soft Arms

A poem for children

Wrinkled and brown like an old paper bag,
Abuelita smiles with her too-perfect white teeth,
And she calls out as I run from Papa's old, gray station wagon,
"Mi cielo, come here! I need a big abrazo from you!"

And I bury myself deep, hidden in Abuelita's soft arms,
Smelling like perfume and frijoles and coffee and candy.

A whole weekend with Abuelita!
I shout, "Bye, Papa!"

Papa smiles and drives off in a puff of white smoke.
I bury my face deeper into her,
Just me and Abuelita,
For the whole weekend.

We march happily into her house
Painted yellow-white like a forgotten Easter egg,
And cracked here and there like that same egg.
But it is her home,
Near the freeway and St. Agnes Church.

On the wall there are pictures of Mama and my two aunts.
And there's one of Abuelita, so young and beautiful,
Standing close to Abuelito on their wedding day.

"Mi cielo," Abuelita says holding my sweaty cheeks in her

Cool, smooth hands.
"You are so big! My big boy!"
And I laugh and stand on my toes to be even bigger.

And I bury myself deep, hidden in Abuelita's soft arms,
Smelling like perfume and frijoles and coffee and candy.

American Heritage Two-Step

Dedicated to those who believe they are monolingual

hacienda

lasso

coyote

San Francisco

arroyo

rodeo

ranch

Toledo

canyon

Los Angeles

barracks

burro

paca

Reading Bukowski in San Pedro

(November 18, 2004)

The meeting had
come to an end,
another public
hearing on seawalls,
endangered species,
developers wanting
their projects along
the California coast.

But now my tie could
come off and my lawyer
duties could be put
in a drawer until
tomorrow when the
Coastal Commission
would reconvene.

I overheard a conversation
as I packed up my
briefcase: "It's the oldest
bookstore in Los Angeles,"
someone said. "Just a
few blocks from here."
My eyebrows popped up,
I smiled. "Really?"

So I walked from the

Sheraton to Williams'
Book Store with another
lawyer who wanted to
get away from her lawyer
duties, too.

We found it after a brisk
stroll along West 6th Street
that November evening.
Established in 1909, the
sign said. Almost a
hundred years old.
Perhaps it was the oldest
in the city.

Small, a bit rundown,
but filled with booksmells,
warm, good. As my
friend wandered deeper
into the store, I stopped
by the first shelf on the
right filled mostly with
Bukowski. San Pedro
had been his home at
the end. So of course
there would be such a
shelf.

As I made my purchase
(*Dangling in the Tournefortia*)
the owner told me

the man himself used
to come by and browse.
And unbeknownst to her, he'd
autograph his books and
slip them back onto the
shelf.

In my hotel room that
night, I sat in my boxers,
pillows propped up behind
me in a bed too large for
for a lone body, and read
about fights and booze
and whores with dirty,
tattered slips and Baby
Face Nelson and more
booze and more whores
and about writing, always
words about writing.

I read and I read
until I could take no more
and I called my wife and
son and told them I loved
them and that I'd see them
the next night after the
three-day meeting was
over.

Morning came and
I shaved,

showered,
drank weak hotel
coffee and entered the
meeting room off
the lobby ready for
another day of public
testimony and quasi-judicial
decision-making of
a state agency.

As a speaker gesticulated
and explained why the
Commission should let
him add a second-story
to his house, I thought
about Bukowski and his
women and fights and
drunken nights.

And I wondered what
he would think if he
were alive, sitting here
in a suit, watching
what I was watching.

Would he be drunk
already, snickering
at the proceedings,
looking to poke a
guy in the eye?

Would he make a
pass at one of the
pretty women in
the audience and
then cuss her out
when she turned away
and vow right there
and then to stick
with whores because
that's the best he
could do and besides
all women were
whores anyway
especially the ones
who didn't want him?
Yes, I think he would
do all that because he was
Bukowski: a bully, a drunk,
a poet.

And as I listened to
the public testimony,
all I wanted to
do was open his book
and get lost in his
tough, sad words again.

Blood, Frogs

Blood, Frogs...
Do you know me, Adonai?
A latecomer to your Seder table?
A visitor waiting for Elijah?

Vermin, Wild Beasts...
You blessed the Moabite,
Ruth, with an honored place
in Ketuvim, so there must be
hope for me.

Pestilence, Boils...
My people have suffered, too,
though nothing like the Inquisition
or the Holocaust. But the Aztecs
were fooled and then slaughtered,
raped and oppressed by
the Spaniards who rode proud horses
roughshod over meso-America
creating a mixed gente,
the Mestizos. And then discrimination,
a glass ceiling we hit, in this great
country, as we scratch toward
the American dream.

Hail, Locusts...
But here I sit, a Jew for only
twelve years, looking at the
matzo, bitter herbs, shank bone,

amidst other symbols of oppression
and subsequent Exodus, Diaspora.
My wife's family (and even my son!)
easy and familiar with it all, as much
a second nature as my Chicanismo
is to me. But each year, I
recognize more and more,
mouthing the Hebrew faster and
faster. Is there hope for this old dog?

Darkness, Slaying of the First Born…
I took the name of Ysrael when
I converted because Jacob wrestled
with the angel and saw the face
of G-d, before he, too, became a
Jew and took a new name.
I wrestled, struggled (did I see
the face of G-d, too?), for over
six years before making the choice.
It is a choice I do not regret, but, at times,
when my ten-year-old son breezes through
the Four Questions in Hebrew (not English!),
I am a stranger searching in bewilderment's
twilight for my soul. Can an outsider
take on another people's traditions,
burdens and history while maintaining
his own proud history?
Can an outsider ever stop wandering?
Will I ever be at home?

The Slack-Jawed Night

The slack-jawed night
sits motionless in
my sorrel leather
chair, not knowing
where he is.

He looks up,
with a jerk of
his head, just
as I move
toward him.

Eyes narrow,
the light bulb
flicks on.

"Ah!" he says.
"Ah, yes!"

I stop short, and
slowly (ever so slowly)
I move back (with a
slight twinge in my
lumbar) and return
to the long, green
couch.

"Ah!" night repeats.
"I am here again!"

"Yes," I answer,
settling into place
and yawning just
a bit. "You are here,
again," I reassure.

Night rubs his rough
chin (he needs a shave,
I believe), and smiles.

"I am better than
nothing," he murmurs,
locking his black,
gleaming eyes on mine.
I force my face
away, to the dusty
crystal sitting unused,
sealed in the mahogany
cabinet that was a wedding
gift almost fifty years ago.
From whom? I don't
remember. But if Lois
were still here,
keeping track of our
lives, she'd know.
She'd know.

"Better than nothing,
eh?" repeats night.

I do not answer.

Night leans forward
(jaw slack no longer, but
now jutting out at me),
fingers intertwined,
brow knitted with
thought. "I am here
for you, now," night
finally says.

I turn and meet his
gaze and nod.

"Yes," I answer
as I rub my eyes.
"You are here,
for me."

La Tormenta at the Lost Souls Café

After the paintings by Gronk

La Tormenta sips a double
Espresso at the Lost Souls Café
Alone on the long, sagging couch,
Listening to the young people
Chatter about art and sex and dogs.

La Tormenta is, of course, young
And rich and beautiful and
Could sit at a fancier café
Surrounded by old men with
Old money, old lies, old desires.

But she does not know who she is,
So La Tormenta continues to sit
In this café off of Spring Street down
An alley where the new loft-dwellers
Come and go, speaking of Michelangelo.

La Tormenta ponders her identity—
Even her name's origin is hidden
In fog and memories of East L.A.
Memories in black and white, not
The Technicolor of Saint Minnelli.

La Tormenta knows a few things:
She has a secret lover named
Isela Boat, one of the infamous

Boat sisters of La Puente, the ones
Who killed their husbands with love.

La Tormenta smooths her black,
Silk dress; she tugs at the ends of
Her long, elbow-length gloves as
She assumes that her adoring fans are
Trying not to disturb her dark solitude.

And La Tormenta doubts that she will ever
Know if her soul is as beautiful as she feels.

Source Acknowledgments

Most of the poems included in this collection were previously published, and are reprinted by permission of the author:

"Why Did You Believe" in *Boardwalk* (2000).

"Writer" in *3rd Muse* (2000).

"Pico Boulevard, October 1972" in *Perihelion* (2000).

"The House" in *Red River Review* (2000).

"Hidden in Abuelita's Soft Arms" in *Love to Mamá: A Tribute to Mothers* (Lee & Low Books, 2001).

"Outside the Box" in *A Writer's Choice* (2001).

"Blood, Frogs" in *RealPoetik* (2001).

"Barrow's Goldeneye" in *bound* (2001).

"Gato" in *Eclectica* (2001).

"A Good Job" and "Green Soldier" in *Red River Review* (2001).

"The Slack-Jawed Night" and "Lindy" in *The TMP Irregular* (2002).

"Western Wallflower" in *The Hornacle* (2002).

"St. Francis Dam, March 12, 1928" in *The Copperfield Review* (2002).

"On the Hill" and "Tezcatlipoca's Glory" in *LatinoLA* (2002).

"Sad Gray House" and "Brown Bomber" in *muse apprentice guild* (2003).

"King," "Crossing the Border" and "Georgina S. Francisco is a Friend of Mine" in *Poetry Super Highway* (2004).

"Papa's Car" and "Reading Bukowski in San Pedro" in *LatinoLA* (2004).

"Woman Gets Probation in Child Neglect Case" in

PULSE (2004).

"Sisyphus Explains" and "West Coast Jazz Marriage" in *The Poetry Victims* (2005).

"Letters to Norco" and "Las Dos Fridas" in *Indiana English* (2006).

"La Tormenta at the Lost Souls Café" in *LatinoLA* (2009).

"¡Xicano!" in *La Bloga* (2011).

"Papa Wrote" in *La Bloga* (2012).

"Slip Dream" and "Wonder Bread" in *Red Savina Review* (2014).

Author's Note Regarding
Accents and Italics

The reader will observe that I do not use accents on the words "Mamá" and "Papá." That is intentional. Though my parents are the children of Mexican immigrants and grew up speaking both Spanish and English, they would refer to themselves as unaccented "Mama" and "Papa." Accordingly, this usage seemed natural to me in writing poems that refer to my parents or that refer to the manner by which our own son refers to me and my wife.

Also, I do not italicize words that are in Spanish. There has been a great deal of excellent discussion on this topic over the last two decades (just Google the phrase "Junot Díaz does not italicize Spanish"), so I will not delve deep into it here. Suffice it to say that italicizing Spanish simply "others" a language that is blended rather easily with English by many people, and I see no reason to stop a line dead in its tracks with an italicized Spanish word or phrase. Besides, in this current political climate, I see no need to build a wall between two languages that have lived side-by-side for a very long time. However, I do use italics for emphasis or as a replacement for quotation marks in certain poems.

About the Author

Daniel A. Olivas is the author of nine books including *The King of Lighting Fixtures: Stories* (University of Arizona Press, 2017), and *Things We Do Not Talk About: Exploring Latino/a Literature through Essays and Interviews* (San Diego State University Press, 2014). He co-edited *The Coiled Serpent: Poets Arising from the Cultural Quakes and Shifts of Los Angeles* (Tía Chucha Press, 2016), and edited the landmark anthology, *Latinos in Lotusland: An Anthology of Contemporary Southern California Literature* (Bilingual Press, 2008). His writing has appeared in many publications including *The New York Times, Los Angeles Times, Los Angeles Review of Books, High Country News, Huffington Post*, and *La Bloga*. He earned his degree in English literature from Stanford University, and law degree from the University of California, Los Angeles. Since 1990, Olivas has practiced law with the California Department of Justice in the Public Rights Division. He and his wife make their home in Los Angeles and have an adult son. Twitter: @olivasdan.